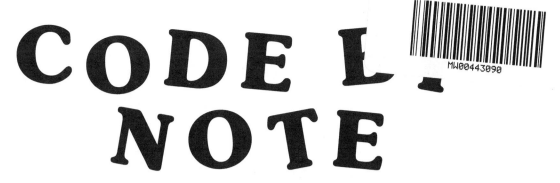

CODE L'NOTE

find the patterns by reading the notes

by SHARON KAPLAN

In this age of spy stories and laser guns, note naming is rather tame and sometimes unexciting stuff. Drill in the form of solving a code will bring intrigue into students' lives. Here are the directions for having your musical "James Bonds" solve the encoded patterns.

The "code book" that precedes each puzzle has specific instructions.
Here is an example.

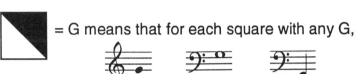

= G means that for each square with any G,

darken the square as shown. Pairs of colors
could be used instead of black and white.

Some codes have different patterns for ♭ C and for 𝄢 C.

In solving the code, the rhythm value of the notes does not affect the placement. The code solving involves only the identification of the letter names.

Two grids are given. One has the notes. The other is a blank grid for encoding the "message" (design).

As an option, students could encode directly over the notes and then use the blank grids to create their own encoded designs. Answers can be found on pages 19 and 20. Have fun!

Sharon Kaplan

By the way, you might suggest using pencil for filling in the answers. It's easy to make mistakes!

Editor: Carole Flatau

2

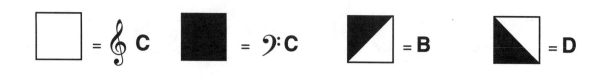

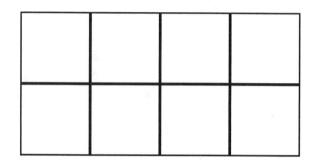

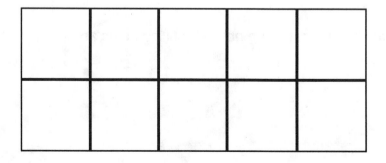

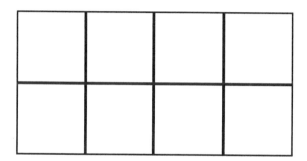

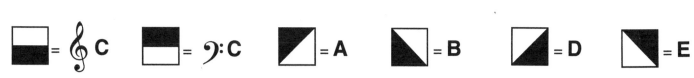

6

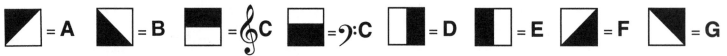

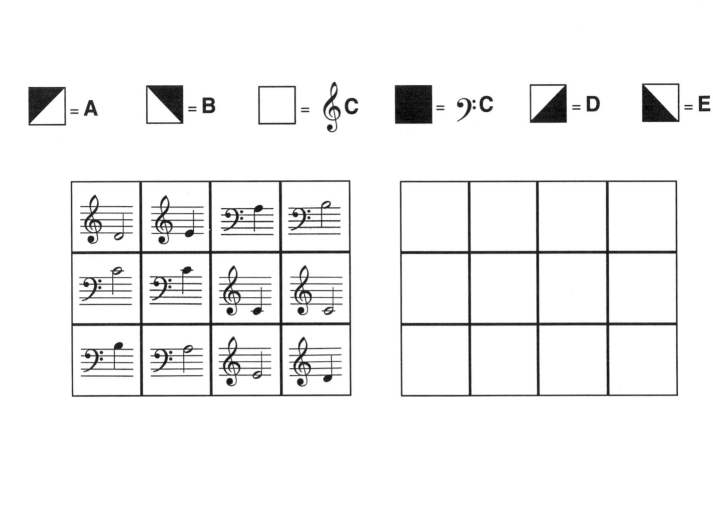

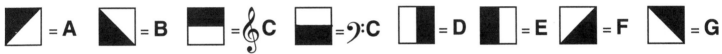

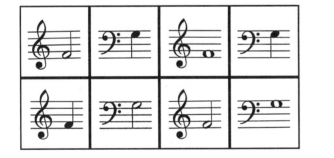

8

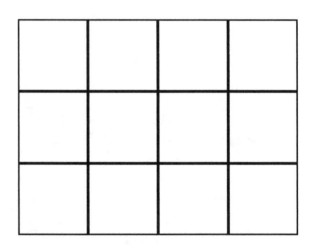

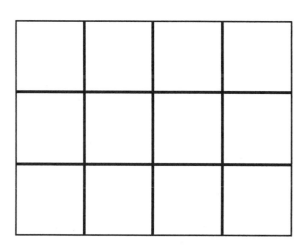

10

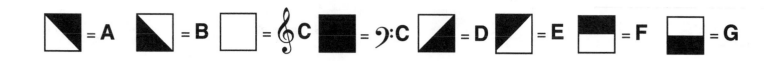

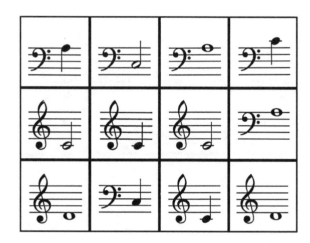 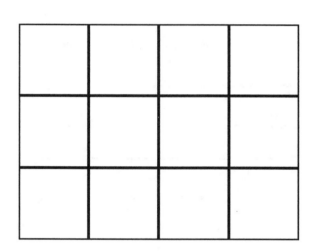

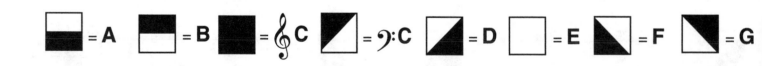

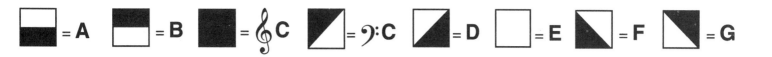

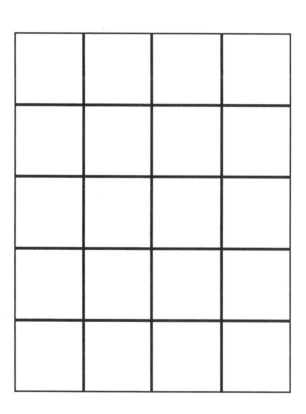

12

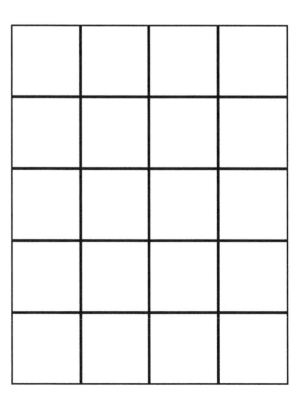

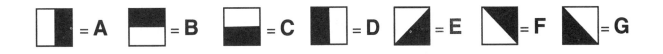

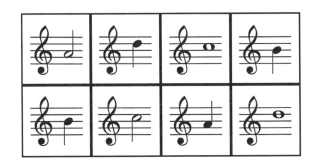

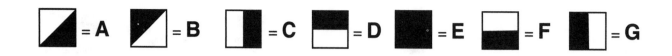

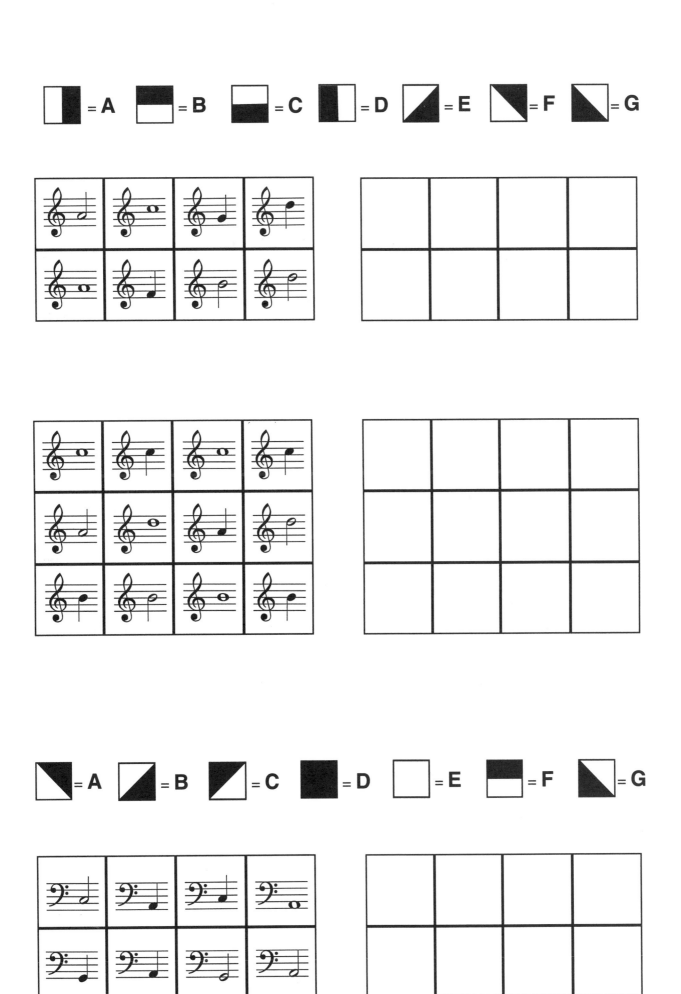

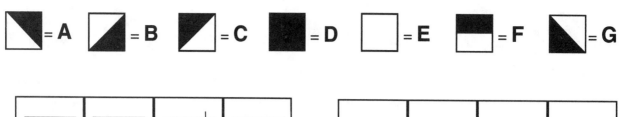

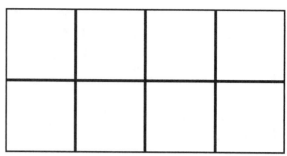

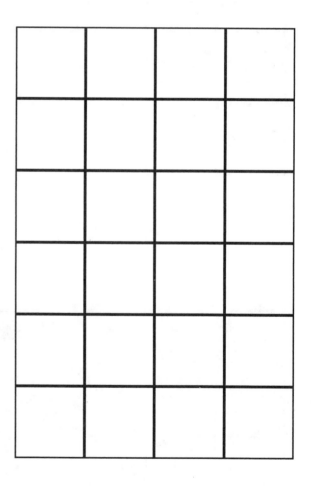

ANSWERS

page
2

page
3

page
4

page
5

page
6

page
7

page
8

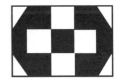

page
9

page
10

20

page
11

page
15

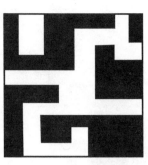 

page
12

page
16

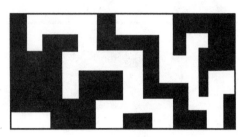

page
13

page
17

page
14

page
18